The
Book
of
Days

The
Book
of
Days

*For birthdays, anniversaries
and special occasions*

Galahad Books · New York

Anniversaries

First	*Paper*		Fourteenth	*Ivory*
Second	*Cotton*		Fifteenth	*Crystal*
Third	*Leather*		Twentieth	*China*
Fourth	*Silk, flowers or books*		Twenty-fifth	*Silver*
Fifth	*Wood*		Thirtieth	*Pearls*
Sixth	*Iron or sugar*		Thirty-fifth	*Coral*
Seventh	*Copper or wool*		Fortieth	*Ruby*
Eighth	*Bronze*		Forty-fifth	*Sapphire*
Ninth	*Pottery*		Fiftieth	*Gold*
Tenth	*Tin*		Fifty-fifth	*Emerald*
Eleventh	*Steel*		Sixtieth	*Diamond*
Twelfth	*Linen or silk*		Seventy-fifth	*Diamond or platinum*
Thirteenth	*Lace*			

Star Signs

Capricorn December 23 – January 20

Aquarius January 21 – February 18

Pisces February 19 – March 20

Aries March 21 – April 20

Taurus April 21 – May 21

Gemini May 22 – June 22

Cancer June 23 – July 23

Leo July 24 – August 23

Virgo August 24 – September 23

Libra September 24 – October 23

Scorpio October 24 – November 22

Sagittarius November 23 – December 22

The Language of Flowers

Almond, Flowering	*Hope*		Mimosa	*Sensitiveness*
Apple Blossom	*Preference*		Moss	*Maternal love*
Bluebell	*Constancy*		Narcissus	*Egotism*
Butterfly Orchids	*Gaiety*		Oak Leaves	*Bravery*
Cactus	*Warmth*		Olive	*Peace*
Carnation, Red	*Sorrow*		Peppermint	*Warmth of feeling*
Clematis	*Mental beauty*			
Daffodil	*Regard*		Plane Tree	*Genius*
Daisy, White	*Innocence*		Poppy, Scarlet	*Extravagance*
Fern, Flowering	*Fascination*		Raspberry	*Remorse*
Forget-Me-Not	*True love*		Rose	*Love*
Gladiolus	*Strength of character*		Rose, White and Red together	*Unity*
			Rosebud, Red	*Pure and lovely*
Gooseberry	*Anticipation*			
Honeysuckle	*Rustic beauty*		Snowdrop	*Hope*
Hyacinth, Blue	*Constancy*		Stock	*Lasting beauty*
Ivy	*Fidelity*		Sweet Pea	*Sweet lasting pleasures*
Jasmine, Cape	*Joy*			
Jonquil	*Wanting return of affection*		Sweet William	*Gallantry*
			Thistle, Common	*Austerity*
Laurel	*Glory*		Tuberose	*Dangerous pleasures*
Lemon Blossoms	*Fidelity in love*			
Lily of the Valley	*Return of happiness*		Violet, Blue	*Faithfulness*
			White Lily	*Purity and modesty*
Lotus Flower	*Estranged love*		Willow, Weeping	*Mourning*
Magnolia	*Dignity*		Zinnia	*Thoughts of absent friends*

January

1

Edward Morgan Forster, English author of *A Passage to India*, born in 1879.

2

Isaac Asimov, American science-fiction writer, born 1920.

3

J.R.R. Tolkein, author of *Lord of the Rings*, born in 1892.

4

Jakob Ludwig Karl Grimm, born in 1785, author with his brother Wilhelm of the classic *Grimm's Fairytales*.

5

Robert Selden Duvall, American actor, born in 1931.

6

7

JANUARY – **Capricorn**
The goat ascending the mountain is an apt symbol of those born under this sign. It reflects the ambitious nature of the Capricorn. Perseverance, patience, adaptability and reliability are typical characteristics.

January

8

Elvis Presley, the legendary American singer, born in 1935.

9

Simone de Beauvoir, born in 1908, noted French author of *The Second Sex* and *The Mandarins*.

10

11

> JANUARY'S GEMSTONE — **Garnet**
> *The gleaming garnet holds within its sway*
> *Faith, constancy and truth for one away.*
> *By her who this month is born,*
> *No gems save garnets should be worn;*
> *They will endure her constancy,*
> *True friendship and fidelity.*

12

Jack London, American writer, born in 1876.

13

Sophie Tucker, American singer, born in 1884.

14

Albert Schweitzer, French philosopher, musicologist and winner of the Nobel Peace Prize, born in 1875.

January

15

Martin Luther King, American civil rights leader, born in 1929.

16

Dian Fossey, naturalist renowned for her work with gorillas in Africa, born in 1932.

17

Benjamin Franklin, American statesman, diplomat, inventor and scientist, born in 1706.

18

A.A. Milne, English author of *Winnie the Pooh*, born in 1882.

19

Paul Cezanne, French impressionist and cubist painter, born in 1839.

20

Joy Adamson, conservationist and author of *Born Free,* born in 1910.

21

Christian Dior, French fashion designer, born in 1904.

January

22

Sir Francis Bacon, English statesman, born in 1561.

23

Eduard Manet, French painter, born in 1832.

24

Desmond Morris, English zoologist and author of *The Naked Ape*, born in 1928.

25

Virginia Woolf, English author of *To the Lighthouse* and *A Room of One's Own*, born in 1882.

26

Jacqueline Du Pré, English cellist, born in 1945.

27

Lewis Carroll, English author of *Alice in Wonderland*, born in 1832.

28

Jackson Pollock, American abstract expressionist painter, born in 1912.

January–February

29

Germaine Greer, feminist and author of *The Female Eunuch* and *The Change*, born in 1939.

30

Franklin Delano Roosevelt, former U.S. president, born in 1882.

31

Anna Pavlova, Russian prima ballerina, born in 1885.

1

Clarke Gable, American actor, born in 1901.

2

James Joyce, Irish novelist and poet, author of *Ulysses*, born in 1882.

3

4

FEBRUARY – **Aquarius**
Guided by reason rather than convention, this sign can produce inspired geniuses and humanitarian leaders. Sociable, progressive and democratic, Aquarians embrace the ideals of liberty, equality and fraternity.

February

5   Bob Marley, Jamaican reggae singer, born in 1945.

6   "Babe" Ruth, legendary American baseball player, born in 1895.

7   Charles Dickens, English author of *Oliver Twist* and *A Christmas Carol,* born in 1812.

8   James Dean, American actor and star of *Rebel Without a Cause*, born in 1931.

9   Sir Charles Kingsford-Smith, Australian aviator and first pilot to cross the Pacific, born in 1897.

10   Boris Pasternak, Russian author of *Doctor Zhivago*, born in 1890.

11   William Henry Fox-Talbot, English 'father of photography', born in 1800.

February

12	Charles Darwin, English naturalist who devised a theory of evolution, born in 1809.
13	Georges Simenon, French author and creator of the Maigret stories, born in 1903.
14	Thomas Malthus, English economist and demographer, born in 1766.
15	Galileo, Italian mathematician and astronomer, born in 1564.
16	John McEnroe, American tennis player, born in 1959.
17	A.B. 'Banjo' Paterson, Australian poet, born in 1864.
18	Helen Gurley Brown, founding editor of *Cosmopolitan* magazine, born in 1922.

February

19 Karen Silkwood, American anti-nuclear activist, born in 1946.

20 Ansel Adams, American photographer, born in 1902.

21

FEBRUARY'S GEMSTONE — **Amethyst**
*The February born will find
Sincerity and peace of mind.
Let her an amythest but cherish well,
And strife and care can never in her dwell.*

22

23 Samuel Pepys, English diarist, born in 1633.

24 Juan Péron, former President of Argentina, born in 1946.

25 Anthony Burgess, English writer, author of *A Clockwork Orange*, born in 1917.

February–March

26

'Fats' Domino, American blues singer, born in 1928.

27

Elizabeth Taylor, English actress, born in 1932.

28

Vaslav Nijinsky, Russian ballet dancer, born in 1890.

29

Gioachino Antonio Rossini, Italian composer of *The Barber of Seville* and *William Tell,* born in 1792.

1

Glenn Miller, American bandleader, born in 1904.

2

Mikhail Gorbachev, former General Secretary of the Communist Party and President of the Soviet Union, born in 1931.

3

Jean Harlow, American movie actress, the original 'blonde bombshell', born in 1911.

March

4

Antonio Lucio Vivaldi, Italian composer of *The Four Seasons*, born in 1675.

5

Rosa Luxembourg, early Russian Communist activist and scholar, born in 1871.

6

Michaelangelo, Italian artist, famous for his 'David' and painting of the Sistine Chapel, born in 1475.

7

8

> ### MARCH – **Pisces**
> *Imaginative and artistic, Pisceans are poets and dreamers who relate to the ideal more easily than the real. Pisceans are particularly successful in the worlds of acting and music.*

9

Vita Sackville-West, English writer and gardener, born in 1892.

10

'Bix' Biederbecke, American jazz musician, born in 1903.

March

11

Douglas Adams, best-selling English author of *The Hitchhikers' Guide to the Galaxy*, born in 1952.

12

Jack Kerouac, American beat poet and author of *On The Road*, born in 1922.

13

Neil Sedaka, American singer, born in 1939.

14

Albert Einstein, American physicist who formulated the theory of relativity, born in 1879.

15

16

MARCH'S GEMSTONE — **Bloodstone**
Who in this world of ours their eyes
In March first open shall be wise;
In days of peril firm and brave,
And wear a bloodstone to their grave.

17

Rudolf Nureyev, Russian ballet dancer, born in 1938.

March

18   Nikolai Rimsky-Korsakov, Russian composer, born in 1844.

19   Wyatt Earp, Deputy Marshal of Dodge City and survivor of the gunfight at the O.K. Corral, born in 1848.

20   Henrik Ibsen, Norwegian dramatist, author of *A Doll's House*, born in 1828.

21   Johann Sebastian Bach, German composer, born in 1685.

22   Marcel Marceau, French mime artist, born in 1923.

23   Sir Roger Bannister, the first man to run a mile in under four minutes, born in 1929.

24   Harry Houdini, American escapologist, born in 1874.

March

25

Gloria Steinem, American journalist and women's rights activist, born in 1934.

26

Tennessee Williams, American playwright, author of *A Streetcar Named Desire* and *Cat on a Hot Tin Roof*, born in 1911.

27

Ludwig Mies van der Rohe, German-born American architect who built the first steel and glass skyscrapers, born in 1886.

28

Raphael, Italian Renaissance painter, born in 1483.

29

Sir Edward Landseer Lutyens, English architect, born in 1869.

30

Vincent van Gogh, Dutch painter famous for his *Sunflowers*, born in 1853.

31

Rene Descartes, French mathematician and philosopher, born in 1596.

April

1
Otto von Bismarck, German statesman, born in 1815.

2
Giovanni Casanova, renowned Italian lover, born in 1725.

3
Marlon Brando, American movie actor, born in 1924.

4
'Muddy' Waters, American blues singer, born in 1915.

5

6

> APRIL — **Aries**
> *The essence of Aries is the life force itself, the desire to be born and the will to survive. Self-reliant, enthusiastic and courageous, Aries is the sign of the pioneer and the leader.*

7
William Wordsworth, English poet, born in 1770.

April

8

Billie Holiday, American jazz and blues singer, born in 1915.

9

Charles Pierre Baudelaire, French poet, born in 1821.

10

Vladimir Lenin, Russian revolutionary leader and head of the Soviet government 1917-24, born in 1870.

11

Sir Charles Hallé, German pianist, conductor and founder of the Hallé Orchestra, born in 1819.

12

Montserrat Caballe, Spanish opera singer, born in 1933.

13

Samuel Beckett, English playwright, author of *Waiting for Godot,* born in 1906.

14

Ortelius, cartographer of the first atlas, born in Antwerp in 1527.

April

15 Leonardo da Vinci, Italian painter, born in 1452.

16 Charlie Chaplin, English comic silent movie actor, born in 1889.

17 J.P. Morgan, American financier, founder of U.S. Steel, born in 1837.

18 Lucrezia Borgia, Italian noblewoman better known as a poisoner, born in 1480.

19 Jayne Mansfield, American actress, born in 1933.

20 Ryan O'Neal, American actor, born in 1941.

21 Catherine the Great, Empress of Russia, born in 1729.

April

22   Sir Sidney Nolan, Australian painter, born in 1917.

23   William Shakespeare, English dramatist, author of *Hamlet*, *Macbeth* and *A Midsummer Night's Dream*, born in 1564.

24   Barbra Streisand, American actress and singer, born in 1942.

25   Ella Fitzgerald, American jazz singer, born in 1918.

26

> APRIL'S GEMSTONE – **Diamond**
> *She who from April dates her years,*
> *Diamonds should wear, lest bitter tears*
> *For vain repentance flow, this stone,*
> *Emblem of innocence is known.*

27

28   Captain Charles Sturt, early explorer of Australia, born in 1795.

April‑May

29
William Randolph Hearst, American newspaper tycoon, born in 1863.

30

1

> MAY — **Taurus**
> *In Taurus, stability and perseverance are blended with an aesthetic sense to produce a slow, steadfast nature with a deep appreciation of beauty and sensuality. Integrity, loyalty and commitment are also characteristics of the Taurean.*

2
Jerome K. Jerome, English author of *Three Men in a Boat*, born in 1859.

3
Golda Meir, former Prime Minister of Israel, born in 1898.

4
Audrey Hepburn, American actress, born in 1929.

5
Karl Marx, German political theorist, born in 1818.

May

6 Sigmund Freud, Austrian psychologist, founder of psychoanalysis, born in 1856.

7 Robert Browning, English poet, born in 1812.

8 David Attenborough, British naturalist and broadcaster, born in 1926.

9 Candice Bergen, American actress, born in 1946.

10 Fred Astaire, American actor and dancer, born in 1899.

11 Salvador Dali, Spanish surrealist painter, born in 1904.

12 Dante Gabriel Rossetti, English pre-Raphaelite painter, born in 1828.

May

13

Daphne Du Maurier, English writer, born in 1907.

14

Gabriel Daniel Fahrenheit, German physicist, inventor of the mercury thermometer, born in 1686.

15

Florence Nightingale, English nurse, born in 1820.

16

17

MAY'S GEMSTONE — **Emerald**
'No other colour is so pleasing to the sight; for grass and green foliage are viewed indeed with pleasure, but emeralds with so much greater delight inasmuch as nothing in creation... equals the intensity of their green...'
Pliny

18

Dame Margot Fonteyn, English prima ballerina, born in 1919.

19

Malcolm X, American civil rights leader, born in 1925.

May

20 Honore de Balzac, French writer, born in 1799.

21 Andrei Sakharov, Soviet physicist and political dissident, born in 1921.

22 Sir Arthur Conan Doyle, British novelist and creator of Sherlock Holmes, born in 1859.

23 Douglas Fairbanks, American actor, star of the *Three Musketeers,* born in 1883.

24 1941 Bob Dylan, American popular musician, born in 1941.

25 Miles Davis, American jazz musician, born in 1926.

26 John Wayne, American actor, born in 1907.

May-June

27   Vincent Price, American horror actor, born in 1911.

28   Patrick White, Australian writer, born in 1919.

29   John F. Kennedy, former U.S. president, born in 1917.

30   Peter The Great, eighteenth century ruler of Russia, born in 1672.

31   Walt Whitman, American poet, born in 1819.

1   Marilyn Monroe, American actress, born in 1926.

2   Thomas Hardy, English writer, author of *Tess of the D'Urbervilles*, born in 1840.

June

3

4

5

Thomas Chippendale, English furniture maker, born in 1718.

6

Bjorn Borg, Swedish tennis player, born in 1956.

7

Paul Gaugin, French painter, born in 1848.

8

Francis Crick, English nuclear biologist, co-discoverer of D.N.A., born in 1916.

9

George Stephenson, English inventor of the steam locomotive engine, born in 1781.

June

10

Judy Garland, American actress and singer, star of *The Wizard of Oz*, born in 1922.

11

Jacques Cousteau, French underwater zoologist and biologist, born in 1910.

12

Anne Frank, Jewish victim of the holocaust, her *Diary* was published after her death in a concentration camp, born in 1929.

13

W.B. Yeats, Irish poet, born in 1865.

14

Che Guevara, Latin American revolutionary theorist and leader, born in 1928.

15

Edvard Grieg, Norwegian composer, born in 1843.

16

Erich Segal, American author of *Love Story*, born in 1937.

June

17 James Brown, American soul singer, born in 1928.

18 'Red' Adair, American firefighter, born in 1915.

19 Duchess of Windsor, American divorcee who married King Edward VIII, born in 1896.

20 Errol Flynn, American swashbuckling actor, born in 1909.

21 Jean Paul Sartre, French philosopher and writer, born in 1905.

22 Billy Wilder, American film director of *Some Like it Hot*, born in 1906.

23 Sir Leonard Hutton, English cricketer, born in 1916.

June

24

Empress Josephine, wife of Napoleon, born in 1763.

25

Antonio Gaudí, Spanish architect, born in 1852.

26

JUNE'S GEMSTONE – **Pearl**

The pearl represents youth and beauty and is a symbol of purity and innocence. It is said that one must be a person of sensitivity and culture to love pearls truly.

27

28

John Wesley, founder of Methodism, born in 1703.

29

Antoine de Saint-Exupéry, French author of *The Little Prince*, born in 1900.

30

Lena Horne, American jazz singer renowned for her rendition of 'Stormy Weather', born in 1917.

July

1　Louis Blériot, early aviator, born in France in 1872.

2　Franz Kafka, Austrian author of *The Metamorphosis* and *The Trial,* born in 1883.

3　Robert Adam, Scottish architect, born in 1728.

4　Guiseppe Garibaldi, Italian patriot and soldier, born in 1807.

5　Jean Cocteau, French film-maker, writer and artist, born in 1889.

6　Fourteenth incarnate Dalai Lama, Buddhist spiritual leader, born in 1935.

7　Ringo Starr, English drummer of The Beatles, born in 1940.

July

8
John D. Rockefeller, American oil billionaire, born in 1839.

9
David Hockney, British painter, born in 1937.

10
Marcel Proust, French author of *Remembrance of Things Past*, born in 1871.

11

12

> JULY — **Cancer**
> *Highly intuitive, sometimes even psychic, Cancer is often the sign of the prophet. Sensitive and emotionally responsive, Cancerians are happiest when they can fulfill their need to nurture and protect.*

13
Harrison Ford, American actor, born in 1942.

14
Emmeline Pankhurst, English suffragette, born in 1858.

July

15 — William Robinson, British horticulturalist, founder of *The Garden* magazine, born in 1838.

16 — Ginger Rogers, American actress and dancing partner to Fred Astaire, born in 1911.

17 — Haile Selassie, last emperor of Ethiopia, born in 1892.

18 — Gilbert White, English naturalist, born in 1720.

19 — Edgar Degas, French painter, born in 1834.

20 — Sir Edmund Hillary, first man to climb Mount Everest, born in 1919.

21 — Ernest Hemingway, American author of *A Farewell to Arms*, born in 1899.

July

22

23

24

Amelia Earhart, American aviator and the first woman to fly solo across the Atlantic, born in 1898.

25

Louise Joy Brown, first 'test-tube' baby, born in 1978.

26

Carl Jung, Swiss psychologist, born in 1875.

27

Alan Border, Australian cricket captain, born in 1955.

28

Beatrix Potter, English author and illustrator of children's stories, born in 1866.

July~August

29

Benito Mussolini, Italian political leader who founded the Italian Fascist party, born in 1883.

30

Henry Ford, American inventor of the 'Model T', born in 1863.

31

Primo Levi, Italian writer, born in 1919.

1

Yves St Laurent, French fashion designer and inventor of the mini-skirt, born in 1936.

2

Peter O'Toole, English actor, 1932.

3

Rupert Brooke, English poet who was killed in the First World War, born in 1887.

4

Percy Bysse Shelley, English poet, born in 1792.

August

5

Neil Armstrong, first man to walk on the moon, born in 1930.

6

Andy Warhol, American pop artist who claimed everyone would be famous for fifteen minutes, born in 1927.

7

Mata Hari, Dutch spy, born in 1876.

8

Dustin Hoffman, American actor, born in 1937.

9

10

AUGUST – **Leo**
With their faith in their own ability, will-power, and flair for attracting attention, Leos are born leaders who will almost always succeed. Generous and noble of spirit, they are also eternally childlike in their fun-loving and joyous approach to life.

11

Enid Blyton, English children's author, born in 1897.

August

12 Cecil B. DeMille, American film-maker, born in 1881.

13 Sir Alfred Hitchcock, American film-maker, born in 1899.

14 Gary Larson, American cartoonist, born in 1950.

15 Napoleon Bonaparte, French military and political leader, born in 1769.

16 Madonna, American singer and actress, born in 1959.

17 Davy Crockett, American frontiersman, born in 1786.

18 Robert Redford, American actor, born in 1937.

August

19	'Coco' Chanel, French fashion designer, born in 1883.
20	Emily Bronte, English writer and author of *Wuthering Heights*, born in 1818.
21	'Count' Basie, American bandleader and jazz musician, born in 1904.
22	Henri Cartier-Bresson, French photographer, born in 1908.
23	Gene Kelly, American actor and dancer, born in 1919.
24	Robert Herrick, English poet, born in 1591.
25	Leonard Bernstein, American composer of *West Side Story*, born in 1918.

August-September

26

AUGUST'S GEMSTONE – **Sardonyx**
Wear a sardonyx or for thee
No conjugal felicity.
The August-born without this stone
'Tis said must live unloved and lone.

27

28

Johann Wolfgang von Goethe, German poet, dramatist and author, born in 1749.

29

Charlie Parker, American jazz musician, born in 1920.

30

Jean-Claude Killy, French downhill skier, born in 1943.

31

Maria Montessori, Italian educationalist, born in 1870.

1

Edgar Rice Burroughs, American novelist and creator of Tarzan, born in 1875.

September

2

Jimmy Connors, American tennis player, born in 1952.

3

Ferdinand Porsche, Austrian automobile manufacturer, born in 1875.

4

Shane Gould, Australian swimming champion, born in 1956.

5

Sir Walter Raleigh, English navigator and historian, born in 1861.

6

Marquis de Lafayette, French statesman and soldier, born in 1757.

7

Elizabeth I of England, born in 1533.

8

Peter Sellers, British actor best-known for his roles as Inspector Clouseau, born in 1925.

September

9 — Captain William Bligh, English naval officer and captain of *The Bounty*, born in 1754.

10 — Sir John Soane, British architect, born in 1753.

11 — D.H. Lawrence, British novelist and poet, author of *Lady Chatterley's Lover,* born in 1885.

12 — Maurice Chevalier, French actor and singer, born in 1888.

13 — Roald Dahl, children's writer, author of *Charlie and the Chocolate Factory*, born in 1916.

14 — Ivan Pavlov, Russian physiologist who discovered the conditioned reflex, born in 1849.

15 — Agatha Christie, prolific British crime writer, author of *Murder on the Orient Express*, born in 1891.

September

16

Lauren Bacall, American movie actress, born in 1924.

17

Stirling Moss, British racing driver, born in 1929.

18

Greta Garbo, Swedish actress, born in 1905.

19

Twiggy, English fashion model in the 1960s, born in 1949.

20

Alexander the Great, 'The Conqueror of the World', born in 356 BC.

21

22

SEPTEMBER – **Virgo**
Virgoans have highly developed critical and analytical faculties. Their sense of order, logic and perfectionism is combined with a desire to be useful. They are are shrewd and exacting, but are also capable of great gentleness.

September

23

Mickey Rooney, American actor, born in 1920.

24

F. Scott-Fitzgerald, American novelist, author of *The Great Gatsby*, born in 1896.

25

Dmitri Shostakovich, Russian composer, born in St Petersburg in 1906.

26

T.S. Eliot, English poet and playwright, born in 1888.

27

28

SEPTEMBER'S GEMSTONE — **Sapphire**
The sapphire is considered the most spiritual of all gems, representing the purity of the soul. It has been known for its healing properties, and its coldness to the touch gave rise to the idea that a sapphire could quench fire. It is the symbol for truth and sincerity.

29

Lech Walesa, Polish labour leader, born in 1943.

September–October

30

Truman Capote, American writer, author of *In Cold Blood*, born in 1924.

1

Julie Andrews, actress and singer famous for her roles in The Sound of Music and Mary Poppins, born in 1935.

2

Mahatma Ghandi, leading figure in Indian independence, born in 1869.

3

James Herriot, English veterinarian and writer, author of *All Creatures Great and Small*, born in 1916.

4

Buster Keaton, American silent movie actor, born in 1896.

5

Bob Geldof, Irish rock star and organiser of Live Aid charity concert in 1986, born in 1954.

6

LeCorbusier, Swiss architect, born in 1887.

October

7

Archbishop Desmond Tutu, anti-apartheid activist, born in 1931.

8

Paul Hogan, Australian actor and comedian, star of *Crocodile Dundee,* born in 1940.

9

John Lennon, English pop musician, member of The Beatles, born in 1940.

10

Guiseppe Verdi, Italian composer of *La Traviata*, born in 1813.

11

Bobby Charlton, English footballer, born in 1937.

12

13

OCTOBER'S GEMSTONE – **Opal**
October's child is born for woe,
And life's vicissitudes must know,
But lay an opal on her breast,
and hope will lull those woes to rest.

October

14

Cliff Richard, English pop musician, born in 1940.

15

Friedrich Nietzsche, German philosopher, born in 1844.

16

Oscar Wilde, Irish poet, dramatist and wit, born in 1856.

17

18

> OCTOBER – **Libra**
> *Engaging, sociable and outgoing, the Libran sense of well-being depends on balance and harmony in their spiritual and physical worlds. Unselfish, objective and impartial, they are able to see both sides of every question. Those born under this sign are often natural peace-makers.*

19

John Le Carré, British spy writer, author of *The Spy Who Came in from the Cold,* born in 1931.

20

Sir Christopher Wren, English architect, born in 1632.

October

21

Alfred Nobel, Swedish inventor and philanthropist who established the Nobel Prizes, born in 1833.

22

Doris Lessing, English writer, author of *Martha Quest* and *The Grass is Singing*, born in 1919.

23

Pelé, Brazilian soccer player, born in 1940.

24

Thomas Gainsborough, English painter, born in 1882.

25

Pablo Picasso, Spanish cubist painter, born in 1881.

26

Beryl Markham, English aviator, born in 1902.

27

Niccolo Paganini, Italian composer and violinist, born in 1782.

October-November

28   Captain James Cook, English explorer and navigator, born in 1728.

29   Edmund Halley, English astronomer, born in 1656.

30   Alfred Sisley, English impressionist painter, born in 1839.

31   John Keats, English romantic poet, author of *Ode to a Nightingale*, born in 1795.

1   Edmund Blunden, English poet, born in 1896.

2   Marie Antoinette, Queen of France who was guillotined for treason, born in 1755.

3   Karl Baedeker, German travel publisher, born in 1801.

November

4

5

NOVEMBER'S GEMSTONE — **Topaz**

Oscar Wilde wrote, 'I have topaz as yellow as the eyes of tigers, topazes as pink as the eyes of wood pigeons and green topazes that are as the eyes of cats'. Considered the stone of strength, deriving its powers from the sun, topaz brings wealth and power and its wearer enjoys long life, beauty and intelligence.

6

Jean Shrimpton, English model in the 1960s, born in 1942.

7

Marie Curie, French scientist who discovered radium, born in 1867.

8

Christian Barnard, South African doctor who performed the first successful human heart transplant, born in 1922.

9

Carl Sagan, American popular scientist and astronomer, born in 1934.

10

Alberto Giacometti, Swiss sculptor, born in 1901.

November

11

Fyodor Dosteyevsky, Russian writer, author of *Crime and Punishment,* born in 1821.

12

Grace Kelly, American movie actress, born in 1928.

13

Robert Louis Stevenson, Scottish writer and author of *Treasure Island,* born in 1850.

14

Claude Monet, French impressionist painter, born in 1840.

15

Georgia O'Keefe, American painter, born in 1887.

16

17

NOVEMBER – **Scorpio**
Resourceful, with the power for regeneration, management and control, Scorpios are often the manipulating force in politics and business. Probing and analytical of others, those born under this sign can also be secretive and intense, revealing little of what goes on under their smooth surface.

November

18
Sir William S. Gilbert, prolific songwriter who, together with Arthur Sullivan wrote *The Mikado* and *Pirates of Penzance,* born in 1836.

19
Indira Ghandi, first woman Prime Minister of India, born in 1917.

20
Nadine Gordimer, South African writer, born in 1923.

21
Rene Magritte, Belgian Surrealist painter, born in 1898.

22
George Eliot, English writer and author of *The Mill on the Floss* and *Middlemarch*, born in 1819.

23
Billy the Kid, American outlaw, born in 1859.

24
Toulouse-Lautrec, French painter, born in 1864.

November

25
Reverend John Flynn, founder of the Royal Flying Doctor service in Australia, born in 1880.

26
Charles Schultz, American cartoonist, creator of the *Peanuts* comic strip, born in 1922.

27
Jimi Hendrix, American singer and guitarist, born in 1942.

28
John Bunyan, English author of *A Pilgrim's Progress*, born in 1628.

29
Gertrude Jekyll, English gardener and horticultural writer, born in 1843.

30
Mark Twain, American author of *Tom Sawyer* and *Huckleberry Finn*, born in 1835.

December

1

Woody Allen, American film director, actor and writer, born in 1935.

2

Georges Seurat, French painter, born in 1859.

3

Maria Callas, American opera singer, born in 1923.

4

Wassily Kandinsky, Russian abstract artist, born in 1866.

5

Constance Spry, English artist, writer and noted flower arranger, born in 1886.

6

Dave Brubeck, jazz composer and pianist, born in 1920.

7

Geoff Lawson, Australian test cricketer, born in 1957.

December

8

Lucian Freud, English painter, born in 1922.

9

John Milton, English poet and dramatist, born in 1608.

10

Emily Dickinson, American poet, born in 1830.

11

Aleksandr Solzhenitsyn, author and Soviet dissident, born in 1918.

12

Edvard Munch, expressionist painter, born in Norway in 1863.

13

14

DECEMBER — **Sagittarius**
The Sagittarian has a wide-ranging spirit which sets its sights on distant shores and is happiest following its own goals, whether personal, spiritual or social. Those born under this sign have enormous mental energy and curiosity about their world.

December

15

Alexandre Gustave Eiffel, French engineer who designed the Eiffel Tower in Paris, born in 1832.

16

Catherine of Aragon, first wife of King Henry VIII, born in 1485.

17

Kerry Packer, Australian media magnate and millionaire, born in 1937.

18

Paul Klee, Swiss painter, born in 1879.

19

Jean Genet, French dramatist, born in 1910.

20

Uri Geller, Israeli psychic, born in 1946.

21

St Thomas à Becket, first English martyr, born in 1118.

December

22

Giacomo Puccini, Italian composer of *Madame Butterfly*, born in 1858.

23

24

DECEMBER'S GEMSTONE – **Turquoise**

The heav'n-blue turquoise should adorn
Those who are in December born;
For they will be exempt and free
From lovers' doubts and anxiety.
No other gem than turquoise on her breast
Can to the loving, doubting heart bring rest.

25

Sir Isaac Newton, English philosopher and mathematician who formulated the law of gravity, born in 1642.

26

Mao Tse-Tung, former chairman of the Chinese Communist Party, born in 1893.

27

Louis Pasteur, French chemist and bacteriologist, born in 1822.

28

Woodrow Wilson, former American president, born in 1856.

December

29
Madame de Pompadour, mistress of French King Louis XV, born in 1721.

30
Rudyard Kipling, English author and Nobel Prize winner, born in 1865.

31
Henri Matisse, French fauvist painter, born in 1869.

Notes

Notes

Styled by Anne-Maree Unwin
Photographed by Andrew Payne

Cover, title page and page 95 photographs styled by Peach Panfili
and photographed by George Seper.

Lansdowne Publishing Pty Ltd,
Level 5, 70 George Street,
Sydney NSW 2000, Australia.

Published in 1994 by

Galahad Books
A division of Budget Book Service, Inc.
386 Park Avenue South
New York, NY 10016

Galahad Books is a registered trademark of Budget Book Service, Inc.

Published by arrangement with Lansdowne Publishing Pty Ltd.

Designer: Catherine Martin (Saggitarius)
Project Editor: Deborah Nixon (Saggitarius)

ISBN: 0-88365-880-1

Printed in Singapore by Tien Wah